the ORIENTAL CARPET IDENTIFIER

CHARTWELL
BOOKS, INC.

A QUARTO BOOK

This edition published by
Chartwell Books Inc.,
A Division of Book Sales Inc.,
110 Enterprise Avenue,
Secaucus, New Jersey 07094

ISBN 1 55521 074 0

This book was designed and produced by
Quintet Publishing Limited
6 Blundell Street, London N7
Picture research: Anne-Marie Ehrlich

Phototypeset in England by
Filmtype Services Limited, Scarborough
Printed in Hong Kong

Contents

ALL THE ILLUSTRATIVE contents and the short introductory texts in this book are derived from my much larger work *Rugs and Carpets of the World*, published now some time ago. That was intended as an authoratative study of the entire field of carpets and other woven pieces produced from very early times up to the present day, and included examples and discussion of European and North American styles and designs in addition to information on Oriental ones.

This book is intended as a guide to the identification of Oriental rugs, carpets and other assorted small woven pieces only. The brief introductions that begin each section outline the reconstructed history of the commencement of weaving in the selected area, the styles of design thereafter, and any influences that affected them. Special motifs are detailed, as is any particular information about colours, techniques and uses; important weaving centres are listed and located; in the section on Later Persian Weaving there is even a brief run-down of names and specific terms. A fairly comprehensive Glossary is also included at the back of the book.

In both this and the larger work, my principal aim has been an attempt to steer a path through the world of carpet scholarship, a world which has an unfortunate tendency to become a morass of conflicting opinions, more likely to confuse the layman than enlighten him. Indeed, carpet books, more than any other form of art history, apparently incline to the view that not only should they be written exclusively by scholars, but read exclusively by them also. The principal difficulty is that there is very little factual evidence of a documentary nature to help us in our search for the origins and derivations of Oriental carpet styles. As far as we can judge, weaving in the Near and Middle East was considered a manufacturing industry and there was no reason, therefore, why details of designs and designers, weavers and manufacturies should be recorded. Thus, the scholar, working with a minimum of hard facts, must perforce erect a hypothetical structure. This is particularly true of Safavid weaving. The trouble is that carpet scholars, with little justification, often consider that their hypotheses are proved, and proceed therefrom with calm assurance and dogmatism. Such scholarship is, in reality, built upon an edifice of shifting sand.

In many respects, our knowledge of carpets has progressed little since the early days of scholarship around the turn of this century. Advances have been made in ethnology, archaeology, and linguistics, which have increased what we know of the life and culture of Eastern kingdoms and empires. Also much study has been done in the last twenty years or so on the techniques of knotting in order to arrive at a more accurate chronology and provenance. This comparatively new science of technical exegesis is still in its infancy, but nevertheless has been responsible for a number of important ideas — the Turkoman 'S-group', for instance, and a critical reassessment of Persian vase carpets.

If there is any area in which modern scholars differ from their predecessors, it is in the moving forward of dates. Many carpets once thought sixteenth- or seventeenth-century are now considered to be eighteenth- or nineteenth-century. The German scholar R. G. Hübel, one of the pioneers of technical analysis, dropped a considerable bomb in 1970 in his study *The Book of Oriental Carpets* (published in English in 1971) when he suggested that even the most 'sacred' of early weavings, the Berlin dragon and phoenix carpet and the Stockhold Marby rug were not, in fact, the fifteenth-century lone survivors of a once great and widespread style, but late seventeenth- or early eighteenth-century copies. As we can see from this and other examples mentioned throughout this book, very little can be taken on trust in the field of Oriental carpet scholarship; and it has to be said that although scholars in fifty or a hundred years time may differ in degree on stylistic attributions or chronology, it is unlikely, without any major archaeological discoveries on a par with that of the Altai Mountains, that they will have any more hard evidence than the scholar of today.

Safavid Weaving

IN 1499, the Safavids began their conquest of Persia. Shah Ismael I was crowned in 1502 and ruled until 1524. He was followed by Shah Tahmasp (1524-76), Shah Ismael II (1576-87), Shah Abbas I (1587-1629), Shah Safi (1629-42) and Shah Abbas II (1642-74). This period, lasting 175 years, was the golden age of Persian art, and carpet weaving was perhaps the greatest of these arts. Major royal factories were established at Kashan, Kerman, Isfahan, Joshaqan and Tabriz. Others were set up at Yezd, Shiraz, Herat and Sabzawar.

The rugs of Safavid Persia have been divided into several categories, based primarily upon the new motifs being introduced at the time, but also in some instances named for historical or technical reasons. The principal categories are the medallion, vase, garden, hunting and figure carpets; other groups are the compartment, large and small silk Kashan, and Polonaise carpets (see below). There are also other groupings of specific types, some of which, like the Portuguese, fall outside any of the above categories, and yet others, like the tree and shrub carpets and the floral Herat carpets, which may be related to the major groups. There are also prayer rugs, which do not, however, form as important a part of Persian weaving as they do of Turkish.

The medallion carpet was one of the earliest of the new designs; many were to be seen at the Shrine of Ardabil before 1600. Arabesques, escutcheons, birds and animals are common on medallion carpets. Vase carpets are directional: they have a right way up, although the vase from which the name derives may be well hidden by rows of floral lozenges or other standard motifs of the period. They are also sometimes described as 'two-' or 'three-plane lattice'. Polonaise carpets form a group dating from the Shah Abbas silk period of Safavid weaving; some were brought to Europe and displayed as part of a Polish collection at the Paris International Exhibition in 1878. An odd group of carpets are the so-called 'Portuguese' pieces which have a huge central medallion either with concentric faceted rims or with very bold floral outlines. In the four corners of the field appear ships, a man in the sea, and fishes; only eight examples are extant.

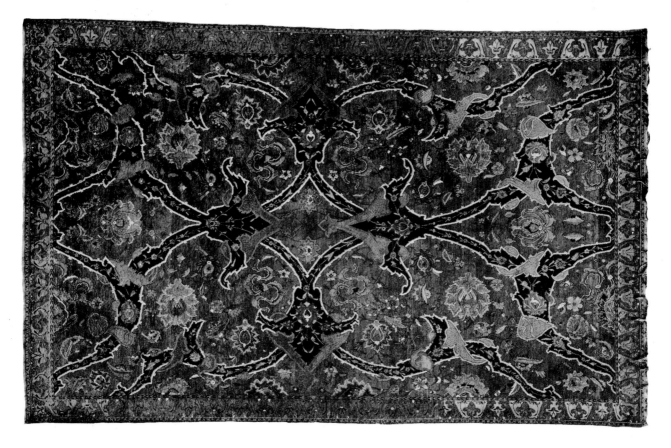

*Above left: floral carpet woven
in the vase-technique. Attributed
by Dimand to Isfahan, early 17th
century. 16 ft. 5 in. × 10 ft. 8 in.
(500 × 325 cm.). Metropolitan
Museum of Art, bequest of
Horace Havermeyer, New York.
Above: multiple medallion and
animal carpet. Probably of the
Sanguszko group, although Dr.
May Beattie claims that it may
be a seventeenth-century copy
woven in a different area.
14 ft. 10 in. × 7 ft. 4 in. (445 ×
220.5 cm.). Duke of Buccleuch
and Queensberry Collection.*

Left:
*arabesque carpet woven in the
vase technique. The wide arabesques are in blue on a red
ground. Possibly Kerman, early
17th century. 11 ft. 10 in. ×
7 ft. 6½ in. (355 × 225 cm.).
Ex-Eric Tabbagh Collection,
Paris; it is now in the Kunst und
Gewerbe Museum, Hamburg.*

Two Shah Abbas silk and metal thread Polonaise carpets. Left: an example dating from the early 17th century. 13 ft. 4 in. × 6 ft. 5 in. (406 × 195.5 cm.).

Above right: the design divides the field into two halves. 6 ft. 9 in. × 4 ft. 9 in. (206 × 145 cm.). Ex-Kevorkian Collection.

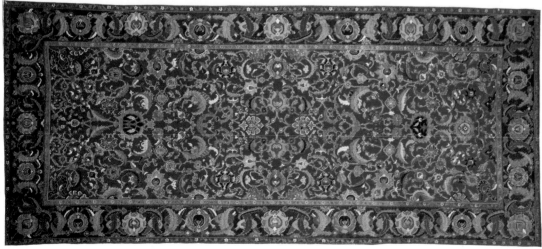

Above:
so-called Indo-Persian animal carpet. Possibly attributable to eighteenth-century Herat. 27 ft. 6 in. × 9 ft. 3 in. (838 × 282 cm.).

Left: floral Herat carpet, late 16th or early 17th century. 16 ft. 2 in. × 7 ft. 1 in. (493 × 216 cm.). Ex-collection of Grace, Countess of Dudley. 9

*Two flat-weave silk and metal
thread Polonaise carpets.
Top: 6 ft. × 3 ft. 6 in. (200 ×
118 cm.). Above: 10 ft. ×
4 ft. 6½ in. (300 × 136 cm.).
Ardabil Shrine Collection.*

Wool and metal thread prayer rug. Many examples of this type are known, including one in the Metropolitan Museum. Although a few writers persist in calling them sixteenth- or seventeenth-century Persian, the majority of scholars are now of the opinion that the rugs are the products of the nineteenth-century Imperial Ottoman factories. 5 ft. 5 in. × 3 ft. 7 in. (162 × 107 cm.). Ex-Paravicini Collection, Cairo. Below: Turkish carpet in silk and metal thread, possibly woven from the same cartoon as the Salting carpet, but slightly later in date, c. 1870. 6 ft. 7 in. × 4 ft. 5 in. (201 × 135 cm.).

*Above: one of a pair
of silk and gold thread
Doria Polonaise carpets, the other
being the gift of John D. Rockefeller Jr. to the Metropolitan
Museum, New York. This piece
is notable for its brilliant colour-
ing and magnificent condition.
13 ft. 8 in. × 6 ft. (410 ×
180 cm.). P. & D. Colnaghi &
Co. Ltd., London.*

*The colour scheme, technique and
character of this garden carpet
indicate that it is actually
Kurdish. 22 ft. × 8 ft. (670 ×
244 cm.). Fogg Art Museum,
Cambridge, Mass. McMullan
Collection.*

Two single-plane lattice vase carpets of the type tradition-ally associated with Joshaqan. Late 18th or early 19th century. Left: 15 ft. 8 in. × 8 ft. 4 in. (477.5 × 254 cm.). Ex-Kevorkian Collection. Below: 15 ft. 10 in. × 6 ft. 6 in. (483 × 198 cm.).

Left : Herat carpet of the so-called 'Isfahan' type, late 17th or early 18th century. 6 ft. 3 in. × 4 ft. 2 in. (190.5 × 127 cm.). Ex-Kevorkian Collection.

Right :floral carpet, wool with silver brocading, Herat, early 17th century. 18 ft. 5 in. × 12 ft. 5 in. (552 × 348 cm.). Shrine Collection, Meshed.

Left : one of a pair of wool and silver brocade carpets with a silk foundation, from the Ardabil Shrine, the other in the Rockefeller Collection, New York. Probably late sixteenth-century Kashan. 11 ft. 7½ in. × 5 ft. 11 in. (327.5 × 175 cm.). Metropolitan Museum of Art, New York.

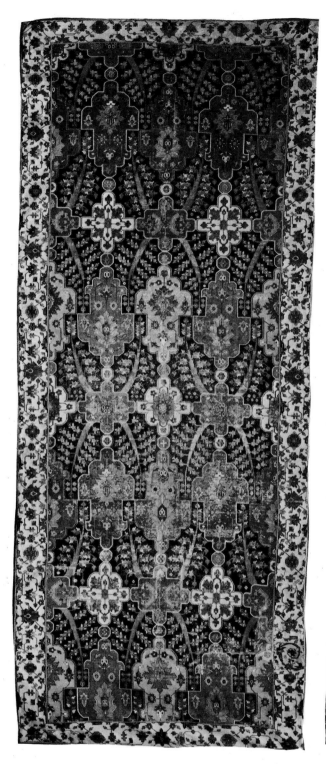

Two tree carpets of the shield type, north-west Persian, late 18th century. Left: complete carpet with an exceptionally beautiful white ground and floral border. 20 ft. 8 in. × 8 ft. 8 in. (634 × 234 cm.). Private collection, England. Right: reduced in length, and with the usual palmette and leaf border. 16 ft. 4 in. × 9 ft. 1 in. (490 × 277 cm.). McIlhenny Collection, Philadelphia Museum.

Directional shrub carpet with lattice. Probably the finest existing carpet of its type. Possibly Kerman, 17th century. 11 ft. 6 in. × 9 ft. 5 in. (351 × 287 cm.). Ex-collection of Grace, Countess of Dudley.

Carpet with a directional design of trees, shrubs and animals. Attributed by Dimand to Kerman, although the borders are reminiscent of carpets attributed to Tabriz. Late 17th or early 18th century. 26 ft. 8 in. × 10 ft. 9 in. (813 × 328 cm.). Ex-Kevorkian Collection.

Floral Herat rug of the Isfahan type, late 17th or early 18th century. 5 ft. 8 in. × 4 ft. 5 in. (173 × 135 cm.).

Early Ottoman Weaving

AROUND 1300, Othman — founder of the Ottoman dynasty and one of several petty rulers who presided over the decline of Seljuk power — unified the country under his capital Bursa (or Brusa). The earliest carpets from the Ottoman period date from a century later, the two most famous of which are the dragon and phoenix carpets now in the Berlin Museum and the Marby rug presently in the Historiske Museum in Stockholm. Both are already stylized, for, as with purely abstract motifs found in Seljuk pieces, evidence of the depiction of animals and birds in Turkish weaving considerably antedates them. Some such evidence is constituted by a number of European paintings of between 1350 and 1450, depicting four principal types of carpet: those portraying heraldic animals and birds; groups of animals, sometimes in combat; pairs of facing birds; and single standing beasts within octagons.

During the second half of the 15th century, the depiction of merely geometrically-patterned pieces became more frequent, especially including variants on the octagon within the style that came to be known as Holbein carpets, or the contrasting octagons and foliate crosses of the Lotto pattern.

Several important innovations were effected at Ushak, in western Turkey, in the production of carpet styles in the 16th and 17th centuries. Five principal new designs emerged: the double-ended mihrab prayer rugs; star pattern rugs; medallion pattern carpets; so-called bird pattern; and the so-called balls and lines (or balls and stripes or Arms of Tamerlaine) pattern.

Small bird Ushak with a white ground. Late 17th or early 18th century. 5 ft. 10 in. × 4 ft. 8 in. (178 × 142 cm.).

Ushak prayer rug. Probably the finest surviving example of its type. Early 16th century. 5 ft. 11 in. × 3 ft. 11 in. (180 × 120 cm.). Islamische Museum, Berlin.

Left: two arabesque or Lotto pattern rugs, showing the coarsening of the design in later pieces. Far left: early to mid-17th century. 5 ft. 7 in. × 4 ft. 3 in. (170 × 129.5 cm.). Left: late 17th century. 5 ft. 3 in. × 4 ft. (160 × 122 cm.).

Far left: detail of a large pattern Holbein carpet, with four octagons within squares on the long axis. 16th century. 14 ft. 4 in. × 6 ft. 8 in. (430 × 200 cm.). Islamische Museum, Berlin. Left: large arabesque or Lotto carpet. Late 16th or early 17th century. 12 ft. 3 in. × 7 ft. ½ in. (369 × 211 cm.). Islamische Museum, Berlin.

19

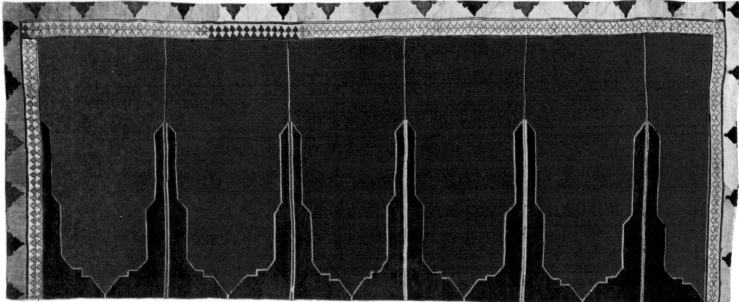

Top:
Small Ushak medallion carpet.
First half of the 17th century.
9 ft. 9 in. × 6 ft. 6 in. (297 ×
198 cm.).

Above:
Saph, probably Ushak, dating
from the early 17th century.
10 ft. 11½ in. × 4 ft. 3 in. (329
× 128 cm.). Islamische Museum,
20 *Berlin.*

The Berlin dragon and phoenix carpet. Although generally considered complete (except for the right-hand border), this may well be a fragment of a much larger carpet. It was discovered by Wilhelm von Bode in a central Italian church in 1886 and is usually dated to early fifteenth-century Anatolia. Its date has recently been questioned by Hübel and others. 5 ft. 9 in. × 3 ft. (172 × 90 cm.). Islamische Museum, Berlin.

Mamluk and Ottoman Weaving in Egypt

SCHOLARSHIP SURROUNDING EGYPTIAN carpets is far from definitive. Four problem areas remain sharply outlined. When were the Mamluk geometric carpets woven — was it in fact during the Mamluk (Turkish-Ottoman) occupation of Egypt at all? Were the so-called Cairene court carpets actually produced in Cairo, which was, after all, the main Mamluk weaving centre of the area and home of certain specific designs and the Senneh knot? Is there any distinction to be made between places of manufacture for the Cairene court carpets woven on wool and those which, woven on silk, also used undyed cotton in the white areas of the design? And finally, where do the compartment rugs — those enigmatic medallion rugs with stylistic similarities both to Mamluk and to Holbein and Lotto carpets, but in structure and coloration different in at least one major variety from anything Egyptian — fit in?

On the first point, scholarship is divided between the traditional view that the Mamluk carpets were woven during the late 15th and early 16th centuries, and that they derive from the first years of the Ottoman domination, from about 1520 through into the late 17th century. These are the carpets which some scholars have associated with the Damascene carpets mentioned in Italian inventories.

The authorities Bode and Kühnel give what is perhaps the best description of Mamluk design in describing it as 'a kaleidoscope translated into textile form'. The usual format is a central medallion, frequently consisting of an octagon, a square and a diamond superimposed. The rest of the field is divided into smaller units containing stars, octagons and stylized floral motifs, arranged around the large central design. The borders usually have a system of alternating oblong cartouches and rosettes.

Above left: an unusual Ottoman Cairene court carpet with a marked abrash. Late 16th or early 17th century. 8 ft. 2 in. × 7 ft. 7 in. (249 × 231 cm.).

Above: a rounded octagonal carpet of Ottoman Cairene design, probably made in Istanbul. Mid-16th century. A round carpet of Mamluk design is in the Barbieri Collection, Genoa. 8 ft. 7 in. × 7 ft. 4 in. (262 × 223.5 cm.). W. A. Clark Collection, Corcoran Gallery of Art, Washington.

Above: Mamluk medallion carpet. Late 15th century. 6 ft 1 in. × 5 ft. (185.5 × 152.5 cm.). Victoria and Albert Museum, London.

*Above left and right
(detail): the Simonetti carpet.
Probably the finest extant example
of Mamluk weaving, and a
brilliant example of the geometric
formalism associated with
Egyptian rugs. 15th century.
29 ft. 5 in. × 7 ft. 10 in. (897 ×
239 cm.). Metropolitan Museum
of Art, New York, Fletcher
Fund.*

The Ottoman court carpet at its most refined and elegant; the vivid but soft green is typical of the carpets in this group. Early 17th century. Probably Istanbul or Bursa. 8 ft. 3 in. × 6 ft. 7 in. (251.5 × 200.5 cm.).

Early seventeenth-century Ottoman court floral rug attributed to Cairo or Istanbul. 6 ft. 2 in. × 4 ft. 5 in. (188 × 135 cm.). Ex-Kevorkian Collection.

*Ottoman court floral carpet.
Probably made in Istanbul or
Bursa. 5 ft. 5 in. × 4 ft. 6 in.
(195.5 × 137 cm.).*

Below: Mamluk medallion rug. A number of examples with a single geometric system have survived. Late 15th or early 16th century. 6 ft. 10 in. × 4 ft. 8 in. (208 × 142 cm.).

Rugs and Carpets of Moghul India

ON HIS RETURN to India from exile, Humayan — son of Babur, the first Moghul Shah — brought with him two of the leading Persian court painters and a love of art and artisanship. Humayan's son, Akbar the Great (1556-1606), went on to establish craft workshops for all artistic productions, including carpets, at centres such as Joshaqan, Khuzistan, Kerwan and Sabzewar, and particularly Herat. To the Persian style, the Indian influence added freedom and aspects of asymmetry, often including animals both real and imaginary in some profusion, although the majority of extant Moghul carpets are of a formal floral design.

Some of the latter were produced on commission for the European market, and incorporated heraldic motifs requested by the commmissioners. A special feature of 17th-century Moghul art was a passion for realism in the flowers depicted. In general, however, there are four main types of Moghul floral rugs. One has a lattice pattern comprising a white trellis on which blossoms or shrubs hang; a common variant on this has a similar lattice, but in abstract form, with colourful flowers on a red background. The second type, associated with the 'Lahore' carpets preserved in the Jaipur Museum, has directional rows of whole plants on a red background. The third type exhibit Persian influences to a far greater degree; and the fourth comprise the prayer rugs, most of which again have rich crimson backgrounds.

Above, top: detail of a
large Moghul carpet with
directional rows of flowering
plants. Mid-18th century.
27 ft. 5 in. × 10 ft. (832 × 305
cm.). Ex-Kevorkian Collection.

Far left: the Aynard rug,
a finely knotted prayer rug. First
half of the 17th century.
4 ft. 2 in. × 3 ft. (124.5 ×
90 cm.). Thyssen-Bornemisza
Collection, Lugano. Left:
although rather shattered in the
centre, this piece is the finest of
the surviving single-flowered
prayer rugs. Early 17th century
5 ft. 1 in. × 3 ft. 3 in. (155 ×
99 cm.). Ex-Engel-Gros and
Paravicini Collections.

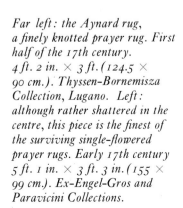

Above:
Detail of a band of cut velvet,
with a design of naturalistically
rendered flowers, typical of
Moghul work. 17th century.
9 ft. 11 in. × 5 ft. 3 in. (298 ×
158 cm.). Victoria and Albert
Museum, London.

Above left: Moghul carpet with directional design of single shrubs. Lahore, period of Shah Jehan, first half of the 17th century. 14 ft. × 6 ft. 7 in. (427 × 200.5 cm.). Formerly in the Kevorkian Collection, now Metropolitan Museum of Art, New York.

Above: detail of an exceptionally large Moghul floral and medallion carpet based on a Persian vase carpet. Period of Shah Jehan. 52 ft. 4 in. × 10 ft. 8 in. (1595 × 325 cm.). Ex-Kevorkian Collection, now private collection, London.

Watercolour of the Girdlers' carpet by Ada Hunter, 1899. This accurate depiction is shown here, since it is not possible to photograph the actual carpet in colour. The original measures 24 ft. × 8 ft. (732 × 244 cm.); it is dated 1634 and is the property of the Girdlers' Company, London. Victoria and Albert Museum, London.

*Above: Indian hunting
carpet of the early 17th century.
Typical asymmetrical design.
8 ft. × 4 ft. 11 in. (244 ×
150 cm.). Museum of Fine Arts,
Boston, Gift of Mrs. F. L. Ames
in memory of Frederick L. Ames.*

*Top: bird and tree carpet known
as the Peacock rug. Possibly
designed by Mansur, court painter
to the Emperor Jehangir. Early
17th century. 7 ft. 10 in. ×
5 ft. 2½ in. (235 × 156 cm.).
Österreichisches Museum für
angewandte Kunst, Vienna.
Above: an almost complete Indian
silk tree carpet, mid-17th century.
12 ft. × 4 ft. 6 in. (360 ×
135 cm.). Musée des Tissus,
Lyons.* 33

Caucasian Weaving

CAUCASIAN CARPETS come from an area of approximately 160,000 square miles between the Black Sea and the Caspian Sea. Although many of the carpets of the so-called 'north-west Persian-Caucasian' group were probably woven inside the present borders of Iran in the region between the towns of Tabriz in the south and Erivan (now called Yerevan) in the north, the majority were woven in, and north of, the regions that used to be called Armenia, Karabagh, Kazak, Moghan and Shirvan, regions now incorporated into the modern Soviet states of Armenia and Azerbaijan. For the purposes of any discussion of Caucasian weaving, however, these older names must be retained.

The carpets of the Caucasus mirror the ethnography of their creators. Until the Russian conquests of the late 18th and 19th centuries, the area had been for over 800 years an ethnic, cultural and religious melting-pot and a ceaseless battleground. Arabs, Tartars, Turks, Mongols, Persians, Russians and others were constantly seeking to make the region theirs, either for political or religious reasons. Both the cultural mix and the barbarism are displayed in Caucasian carpet design.

The earliest Caucasian weavings are the dragon rugs — although the dates and the history of extant pieces are the subject of considerable controversy. Designs are nevertheless based on Persian prototypes involving stylized animals, sometimes in combat, which then assimilated to four Caucasian standard forms. The earliest is least stylized, and has a lozenge-diaper surround of serrate leaves. In the second type, stylization of the dragon is augmented and the lozenge diaper is disintegrating. The third is a further stage of this progression. And in the fourth type, the process has gone about as far as possible: dating from about 1750 to 1850 (and thus relatively common), the format has become pretty well geometric.

The Caucasians also produced floral rugs, generally in Kuba, to the north. Again, the earliest are based on Persian designs, with lattices (such as the Nigde carpet). But there are also tree rugs, and a third type involving rows of individual palmettes, flowers or leaves.

Caucasian weaving of the last two centuries is complex. Although there are inevitable cultural and ethnic overlaps, it is possible to divided the Caucasus into ten weaving areas: Kazak, Karabagh, Gendje, Talish, Moghan, Shirvan, Baku, Kuba, Daghestan and Derbend. It should be noted, however, that the generic name Kazak is often applied to a wide variety of Caucasian rugs not necessarily woven in the Kazak district.

Right: floral carpet (detail) of the shield group. Kuba or Shirvan, late 18th or early 19th century. 9 ft. × 5 ft. 3 in. (274 × 160 cm.). Far right: floral rug. Kuba or Shirvan, twentieth-century copy. 9 ft. 2 in. × 5 ft. 10 in. (279 × 178 cm.).

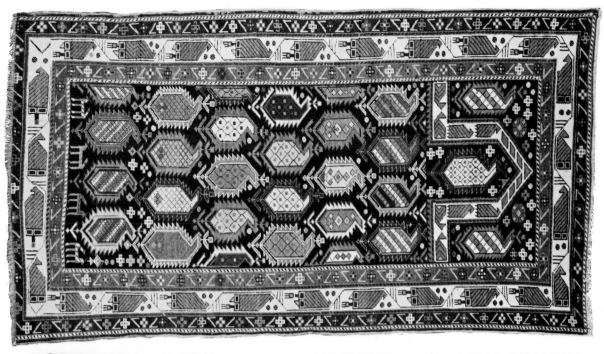

Top: prayer rug, probably Chan Karabagh, but possibly Marasali. Early 19th century. 6 ft. 2 in. × 3 ft. 4 in. (188 × 110 cm.). Above: Karabagh rug; late 19th or early 20th century. 6 ft. 10 in. × 4 ft. 9 in. (208 × 145 cm.). Left: detail of a Karabagh corridor carpet in the European taste. Dated A.H. 1294 (A.D. 1877). 15 ft. 9 in. × 5 ft. 4 in. (480 × 162.5 cm.).

Moghan rug. 19th century. 6 ft. 11 in. × 4 ft. (211 × 122 cm.).

35

Late eighteenth-century hunting carpet. Possibly southern Caucasus, but probably Kurdistan. 12 ft. 8¾ in. × 6 ft. 2¼ in. (386.5 × 188.5 cm.). Metropolitan Museum of Art, New York. Gift of Joseph V. McMullan.

Two Kazak prayer rugs. Right:
5 ft. 5 in. × 4 ft. 7 in. (165 ×
139.5 cm.). Below: 4 ft. 11 in. ×
3 ft. 7 in. (150 × 109 cm.).

Three Kazak rugs. Above: the
type called Sewan Kazak by
German scholars. Late 19th
century. 7 ft. 4 in. × 6 ft. 4 in.
(230.5 × 193 cm.). Right:
possibly Schulaver. 19th century.
8 ft. 2 in. × 4 ft. 6 in. (249 ×
137 cm.). Far right: Karatchoph
rug, probably late 19th or
early 20th century.
7 ft. 5 in. × 5 ft. 1 in.
(226 × 155 cm.).

*Above: Talish rug of typical
design; mid-19th century;
7 ft. 6 in. × 3 ft. 1 in. (228 ×
94 cm.).*

*Top: Shirvan rug from
Chajli; late 18th or early
19th century. 7 ft. 7 in. ×
4 ft. 3 in. (231 × 129.5 cm.).
Above middle:
Shirvan rug, possibly from
Marasali; late 19th century;
6 ft. 1 in. × 5 ft. 5 in. (185.5 ×
104 cm.).*

*Above: Shirvan rug of the type
called Akstafa. Late 19th
century. 8 ft. 2 in. × 3 ft. 11 in.
(249 × 119 cm.).*

*Kurdish copy of a Caucasian dragon rug. Signed 'Hasan Beg'
and dated 'Muharram A.H. 1011' (October, A.D. 1689),
14 ft. 6 in. × 6 ft. (453 × 180 cm.). Textile Museum,
Washington.*

Above:
Floral carpet traditionally attributed to Kuba, but possibly Shirvan or Shusha. 17th or 18th century. 9 ft. 11 in. × 7 ft. 10 in. (302 × 239 cm.).

Left:
Kuba rug from the village of Chichi. The slanting band and rosette border is a characteristic feature. Early 19th century. 4 ft. 6 in. × 3 ft. 2 in. (137 × 96.5 cm.).

Below, top, left to right: Kuba rug from Perepedil; dated three times at the top in the Christian calendar, 1901; 6 ft. 10 in. × 5 ft. 5 in. (208 × 165 cm.). Kuba rug from the village of Chichi; 10 ft. 8 in. × 5 ft. 4 in. (325 × 162.5 cm.). Star Kuba floral runner dated A.H. 1301 (A.D. 1884); 14 ft. 2 in. × 4 ft. (432 × 122 cm.). Below, bottom, left to right: Kuba rug from Perepedil; dated in both the Christian and Islamic calendars, A.H. 1324 and A.D. 1906; 6 ft. 6 in. × 4 ft. 1 in. (198 × 124 cm.). Kuba rug possibly from Konagend; second half of the 19th century; 5 ft. 11 in. × 4 ft. (130 × 122 cm.). Karabagh floral rug from Chila; 19th century; 8 ft. 4 in. × 3 ft. 8 in. (254 × 112 cm.).

Below:
Kuba prayer rug close in design to Daghestan pieces. 19th century, 5 ft. × 3 ft. 4 in. (152.5 × 101.5 cm.).

Below: Armenian Kazak rug dated in Western Arabic numerals A.D. 1890. 7 ft. 4 in. × 4 ft. 3 in. (213 × 129 cm.). Below centre: Karabagh rug from Chondzoresk of the type once called 'cloud-band Kazak'. Early 19th century. 8 ft. 5 in. × 5 ft. 5 in. (257 × 165 cm.).

Above: Baku rug of the type known in the trade as 'Boteh-Chila' (or 'Hilah'). 19th century. 12 ft. 5 in. × 5 ft. 3 in. (377 × 160 cm.).
Left:
Kuba rug of Lesghi design, with the typical stars associated with Lesghistan tribal weaving. Mid-19th century. 5 ft. 8 in. × 4 ft. 7 in. (173 × 140 cm.).

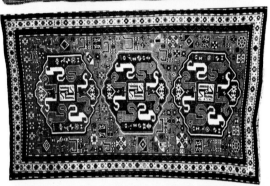

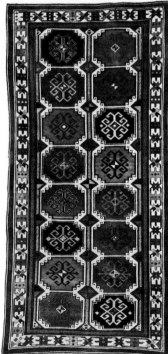

Above:
Moghan rug. The characteristic layout of two rows of hooked octagons should be compared with the motifs found on carpets in early Flemish paintings. Early 19th century. 8 ft. 6 in. × 4 ft. 1 in. (259 × 124 cm.).

Above centre:
Kazak rug of the type attributed to Bordjalou. Late 18th or early 19th century. 7 ft. × 4 ft. 1 in. (213.5 × 124.5 cm.).
Above: pictorial rug attributed to Shirvan, but possibly Kurdish, c. 1880. 5 ft. 7 in. × 3 ft. 9 in. (170 × 140 cm.).
Left: Karabagh carpet made for the Western market. 19th century. 18 ft. 9 in. × 7 ft. 1 in. (570 × 216 cm.).

Karabagh rug from Chelaberd,
of the type called 'eagle Kazak'.
Mid-19th century. 7 ft. ×
44 *4 ft. 10 in. (208 × 147.5 cm.).*

Below: Kazak rug of the type
attributed to Lori-Pambak.
Late 19th century. 8 ft. 8 in. ×
6 ft. (264 × 183 cm.).

Above: The Nigde carpet (detail).
Traditionally attributed to Kuba,
but possibly Shirvan or Shusha.
Early 17th century. 24 ft. 8 in. ×
10 ft. (752 × 305 cm.). The
Metropolitan Museum of Art,
New York, Gift of Joseph V.
McMullan.

Weaving of the Turkoman and Baluchi Tribes

TURKOMAN WEAVINGS were produced mainly in the three Soviet states of Turkimenistan, Karakalpakstan and Uzbekistan. The primary influences on the life and culture of these warlike regions have been Mongolian and Turkish, and many of the motifs found in Turkoman weavings can be traced to these sources.

The origins of existing Turkoman weaving are a matter of some controversy. The traditional view was that the Turkomans, essentially nomadic people, used their carpets as functional objects and for no other purpose; the weavings thus had only a short life. Recent scholarship, however, disputes this, for it now seems clear that the Turkomans did regard their weavings with some respect, and wove not only pieces for their tents but also for urban dwellings.

Turkoman weavings have a predominant colour-scheme of red, red-brown and red-blue; the principal motif is the 'gul' (or ghul, ghol or gol), an octagon or a variant on the octagon, containing other, smaller motifs, that may represent a highly formalized flower and that is quite likely also to relate to one specific Turkoman tribe. The main tribes are the Tekke (the largest), the Yomut, the Salor (the oldest), the Saryk, the Chaudor (or Chodor), the Ersari and their sub-tribes of the Beshir, Kizil-Ayak and the Arabatchi, and the Karakalpak. After 1884, many Turkoman tribes also set up bases in Afghanistan.

Like the Turkomans, the Baluchi tribes generally wove small pieces and bags for use in desert living. A poor people, their main weaving area straddles the Persian-Afghan border for some 300 miles, their main market-place the town of Torbat in the north, 60 miles south of Meshed.

Baluchi wool is especially soft; colours are deep and rich. There is no specific Baluchi design, except that they are fond of tree-of-life motifs; the primary influence is Turkoman.

Late nineteenth-century Yomut horse cover (at-djoli). *7 ft. 6 in. × 6 ft. 5 in. (229 × 196 cm.).*

Although described by previous writers as *Yomut* or *Kizil-Ayak*, technical analysis has proved that the rare and beautiful prayer rugs of the type illustrated here should be ascribed to the Arabatchi. *Second half of the 19th century. 4 ft. 8 in. (142 cm.) square.*

Below: a late nineteenth-century or early twentieth-century *Pende* juval *face, adopting the Salor turreted gul. 5 ft. 9 in. × 3 ft. 4 in. (175 × 102 cm.).*

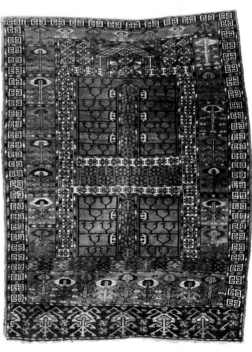

Above: *Tekke* engsi, *of the type called* hatchli. *Late 19th century. 5 ft. 3 in. × 4 ft. 3 in. (165 × 129 cm.).*

Modern 'black' Baluchi carpet with a design of conjoined diamonds, possibly adapted from Beshir weaving. 7 ft. 7½ in. × 4 ft. 9 in. (231.5 × 144.5 cm.).

Baluchi prayer rug with typical tree-of-life design in the mihrab. Late 19th century. 5 ft. × 2 ft. 10 in. (152.5 × 86 cm.).

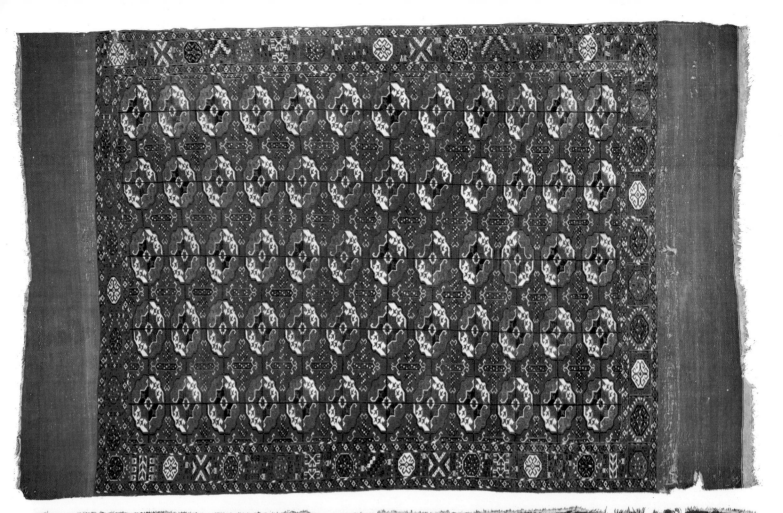

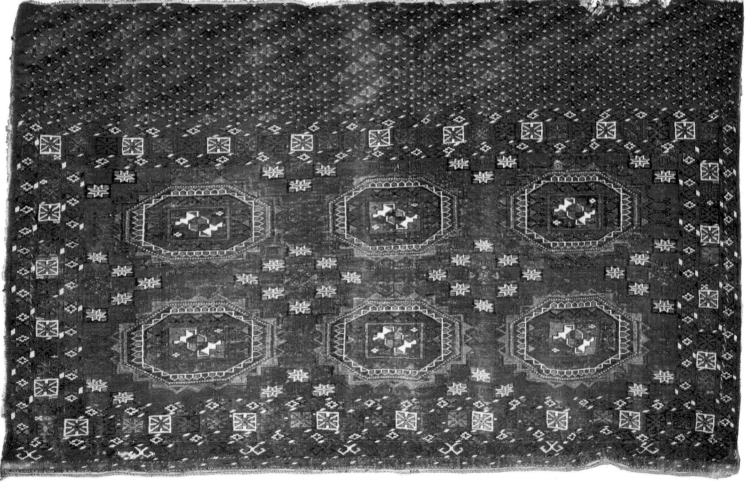

Top:
Tekke carpet. Second half of
the 19th century. 12 ft. ×
5 ft. 9 in. (364 × 175 cm.),
including flat-woven ends.

Above:
Tekke juval face adopting the
Salor turreted gul. Mid- to late
19th century. Approximately
4 ft. × 2 ft. 6 in. (122 ×
76 cm.). Victoria and Albert Museum.

49

Left: Yomut asmalyk or camel flank hanging. Mid- to late 19th century. 3 ft. 9 in. × 2 ft. 5 in. (114 × 74 cm.).

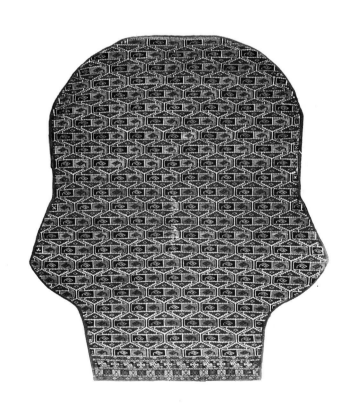

Late nineteenth-century Yomut horse cover (at-djoli). 7 ft. 7 in. × 6 ft. 10 in. (218 × 208 cm.).

Above, left to right: three Beshir carpets. Conjoined diamond design; second half of the 19th century; 7 ft. 10 in. × 4 ft. 7 in. (239 × 140 cm.). Diamond lattice design; early 19th century; 7 ft. 7 in. × 4 ft. 7 in. (231 × 140 cm.). Herati design with octagons; mid- to late 19th century; 11 ft. 2 in. × 5 ft. 6 in. (339 × 168 cm.).

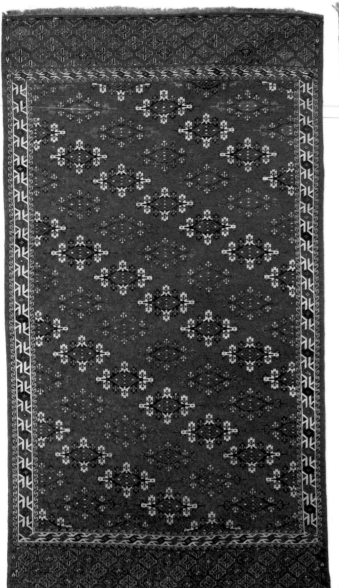

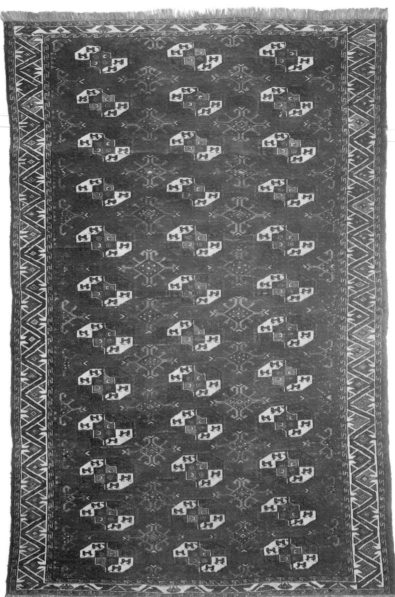

Above: Yomut carpet with kepse guls. Second half of the 19th century. 9 ft. 6 in. × 5 ft. (290 × 152.5 cm.). Above right: Yomut carpet with tauk naska guls. Mid-19th century. 8 ft. 5 in. × 5 ft. 6 in. (256 × 167.5 cm.).

Opposite: Meshed Baluchi rug. The wool of this rug is of exceptional fineness. The design may have been adapted from Beshir weaving. Mid-19th century. 6 ft. × 4 ft. 4 in. (180 × 132 cm.).

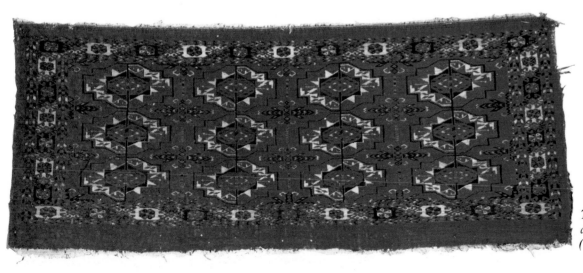

Tekke juval face. Late 19th century. 3 ft. 8 in. × 1 ft. 6 in. (112 × 46 cm.).

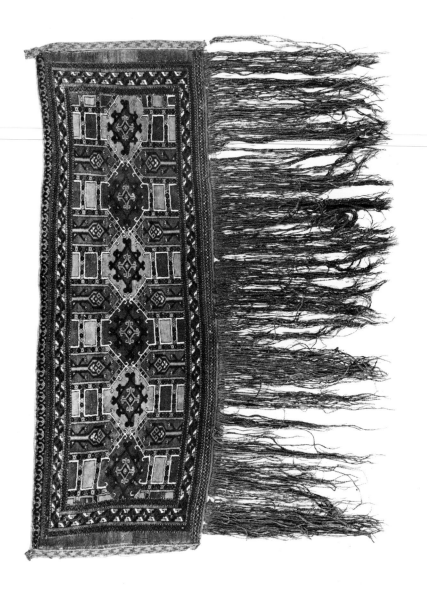

*Above: Afghan Charshango
torba, with dark blue fringes.
Late 19th century. 4 ft. 6 in. ×
1 ft. 8 in. (137 × 51 cm.).
Below right: north Afghanistan
Turkoman prayer rug, dated
A.H. 1342 (A.D. 1925). 4 ft ×
2 ft. 10 in. (122 × 86 cm.).*

*Belutschen-Gebetsteppich,
wahrscheinlich aus Sistan in
Südostpersien, frühes 20. Jh.
119,5 × 76 cm.*

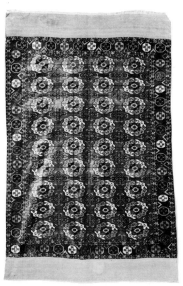

*Afghanischer Wasiri-
Turkmenenteppich, frühes
20. Jh. 160 × 94 cm.*

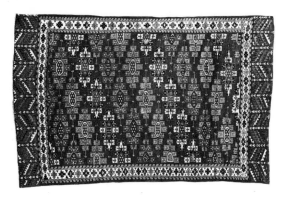

*Top: Tekke carpet; the large
guls indicate a slightly earlier
date than the carpet illustrated
on p. 163. Mid-19th century.
8 ft. 8 in. × 6 ft. 4 in. (264 ×
193 cm.). Above: Ersari carpet
with tauk naska guls. Second
half of the 19th century.
8 ft. 2 in. × 6 ft. 7 in. (249 ×
201 cm.).*

*Yomut carpet with kepse guls.
Second half of the 19th century.
9 ft. 6 in. × 5 ft. (290 ×
152.5 cm.).*

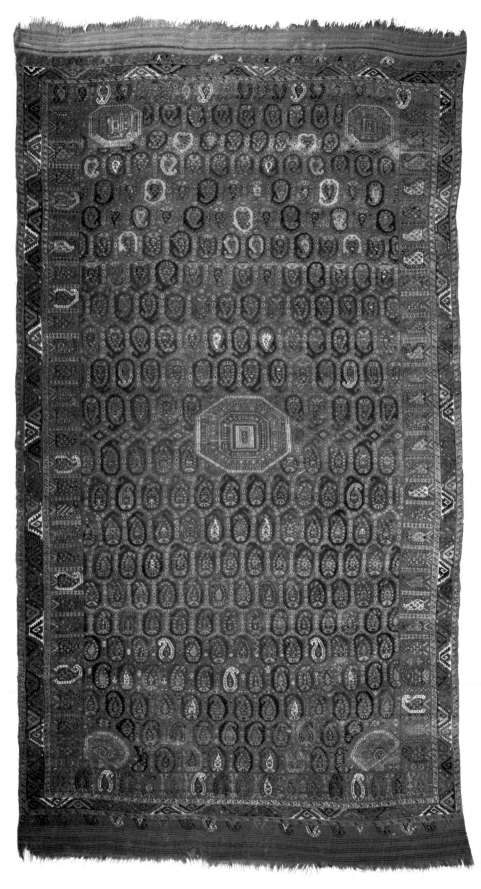

Opposite: Afghan Ersari
pardah *of* hatchli *design.*
Touches of silk in the border.
c. 1900. Approximately 7 ft. 6 in.
× 5 ft. 7 in. (231 × 170 cm.).

Above left: large Beshir carpet
with botehs. *Probably first half*
of the 19th century. 16 ft. ×
8 ft. (488 × 244 cm.). Top
right: Beshir prayer rug. Mid-
to late 19th century. 5 ft. × 3 ft.
(150 × 90 cm.). Above:
Chaudor carpet. Second half of
the 19th century. 9 ft. 2 in. ×
7 ft. 7 in. (275 × 228 cm.).

57

Far Eastern Weaving

THIS SECTION COVERS weaving in Mongolia, Turkestan, China and Tibet.

The first two areas are usually considered together as a region (and sometimes called East Turkestan). It stretches about 1,000 miles from well into what is now the Soviet Union far into China; its principal cities are Samarkand, Tashkent, Yarkand, Kashgar and Khotan, most of which were on the celebrated silk route. Influences were thus many and various, and confusion has been caused even to experts by naming pieces after their places of marketing not manufacture (so a 'Samarkand' can actually have been woven in Khotan). Nevertheless, some authorities ascribe all silk pieces to Khotan, as also those pieces with a design of an all-over lattice and a trellis of stems and flower heads, often on a field of yellow or blue. Brilliant polychrome saphs were produced in Khotan late into the 19th century. The pomegranate rugs — like some of the floral and most of the medallion rugs — usually have one of the three predominant East Turkestan borders: one a series of flower sprays each with three blossoms and in two contrasting colours, another a stylized interpretation of the Chinese wave pattern resembling zigzags surmounted by a sort of ram's head motif, and the third a running T-border also historically derived from Chinese weavings. There are also some highly formalized motifs that some commentators describe as guls and others as medallions.

China was, and is, of course the land of silk. Neither Muslim nor nomadic, the people wove pieces in very different style and for purposes very different from those of East Turkestan, although to some extent historically influenced by Mongolian design precepts. All the same, some design motifs go back over one millennium: birds, shrubs growing from hillocks, clouds, pilgrims, and flowers among arabesques of leaves and tendrils; the Mongolian influence is detectable in an occasionally more geometric style. Many of these motifs had symbolic meanings related phonetically; others were part of Chinese mythology; yet others represented groups of tenets or principles, such as the Eight Symbols of Taoism or the Four Symbols of Gentlemanly Accomplishments (music, chess, poetry and painting). Another group of carpets — mainly from the 19th century — portrays Buddhist themes.

Tibetan weaving is traditionally functional — for sitting and/or sleeping upon, or for use as saddles or animal-covers. Most pieces made as genuine carpets date only from the last 100 years and incorporate foreign design motifs.

Mongol saddle rug, early to mid-19th century. 4 ft. 2 in. × 2 ft. 1 in. (127 × 63.5 cm.). Formerly in the McMullan Collection.

Far left: Khotan carpet with a dark rust-red field, with pomegranate design in blue and white and Yun-Tsai-T'uo border. 19th century. 12 ft. 7 in. × 6 ft. 4 in. (384 × 193 cm.). Left: silk Khotan rug, with an aubergine field and a single pomegranate system. 19th century. 6 ft. 11 in. × 3 ft. 9 in. (211 × 140 cm.).

Above: Khotan carpet with flattened oval medallions and madder-red field. Second half of the 19th century. 11 ft. 4 in. × 6 ft. 2 in. (345 × 188 cm.).

Tibetan medallion carpet. 19th or 20th century. 5 ft. 2 in. × 3 ft. (158 × 91 cm.).

Chinese silk and metal thread carpet, with symbols of the Four Accomplishments. Late 19th or early 20th century. 7 ft. 2 in. × 4 ft. 2 in. (218 × 127 cm.).

Above: the Menasce carpet. Woven in silk and metal thread with Amitabha Buddha seated on the Lotus Throne, Buddhist emblems and four of the Eight Precious Things. Woven with the inscription Ch'ien-ch'ing Kung Yu-yung *(For Imperial Use in the Palace of Cloudless Heaven). Mid-19th century. 7 ft. 4½ in. × 4 ft. ¾ in. (225 × 124 cm.).*

Above: Chinese silk and metal thread carpet woven with inscription Ning-shou Kung Yuan-ko *(Woven for the Palace of Eternal Heaven). Mid-19th century. A hitherto unpublished addition to this group. 8 ft. 1 in. × 5 ft. 1½ in. (246.5 × 157 cm.).*

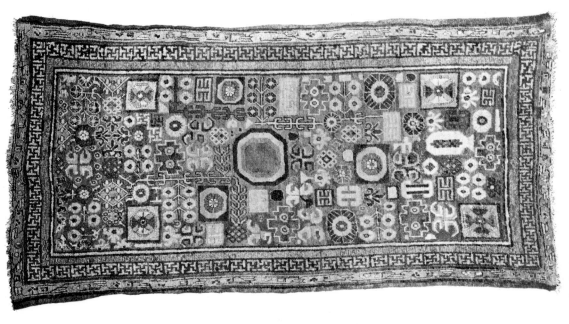

Khotan carpet. Late 19th century. Approximately 11 ft. × 5 ft. (332 × 152.5 cm.).

Silk carpet with pomegranate design and trefoil border. Yarkand or Khotan. Mid-19th century. 11 ft. 11 in. × 6 ft. 4 in. (363 × 193 cm.).

61

Later Ottoman Weaving

WE HAVE ALREADY SEEN examples of earlier Ottoman weaving design — the Lotto, the star Ushak, the balls and stripes Ushak, the Cairene floral carpet, the bird Ushak and the Holbein carpets — and noted the production of prayer rugs. Motifs remained fairly constant in the succeeding centuries, although styles tended to formalize and simplify gradually.

The town of Ghiordes was the most prolific in producing prayer rugs, generally in one of two principal styles: one has a plain red mihrab, a horseshoe-shaped arch from which hangs a schematized mosque lamp, and sometimes formalized columns; the other, more common type has a mihrab that is squarish, with shoulders and a V-shaped arch, and is usually dark blue, red, buff, cream or white, with an elaborate system of floral borders imparting a lacy, almost feminine, effect. There are other Ghiordes designs, mostly incorporating the small, hollow circular motifs called *sinekli* (fly-specks), occasionally with the black and white striped *cubukli* border.

Prayer rugs from Ladik commonly have a triple-arched design with supporting columns generally on a red background. More recent pieces reduce the number of columns to two and create an altogether longer, thinner design. Most Bergama rugs — made in Transylvania — have double-ended buff, red or cream-coloured Ushak mihrabs with central medallions, with one or two principal sets of further motifs: either an arabesque of stems with large flowers and a stylized mosque lamp at both ends, or short poles at both sides of the large central medallion. Many similar pieces, however, have been produced in the Caucasus.

Other village designs include that of a square red field containing two octagons each containing smaller octagons, blue bars, red geometric hooks, and stars, altogether suggesting the quality of stained glass. Most prolific of the lesser villages were Konya, Kula, Kakri, Melas and Kirshehir, and equally productive were the nomadic tribes known as Yuruks. Many of these pieces tend to avoid the colour blue.

Nineteenth and 20th-century weaving in Turkey has been concentrated on the town of Hereke and the Istanbul suburb of Koum Kapou, but is almost entirely derivative in style, based on earlier Ottoman or even Safavid designs.

Opposite, top left: late eighteenth-century Ghiordes prayer rug with sinekli *decorated mihrab and* çubukli *borders. 4 ft. 7 in. × 3 ft. 7 in. (140 × 109 cm.). Opposite, top right: nineteenth-century Panderma prayer rug in the Ghiordes style. 5 ft. 4 in. × 4 ft. 1 in. (152 × 124 cm.). Opposite, bottom left: late eighteenth-century Kis Ghiordes prayer rug. 5 ft. 8 in. × 4 ft. 3 in. (172.5 × 129 cm.). Opp. bottom right: late nineteenth-century Persian silk prayer rug from Tabriz in Ghiordes style. 5 ft. 6 in. × 3 ft. 11 in. (168 × 119 cm.).*

Far left: 19th-century Koum Kapou silk and metal thread prayer rug of the so-called Safavid type. 5 ft. 10 in. × 3 ft. 11 in. (178 × 120 cm.). Left: Hereke wool pictorial rug. Late 19th or early 20th century. 6 ft. 3 in. × 4 ft. (191 × 122 cm.).

*Top: Bergama Transylvanian
prayer rug. Late 17th century.
5 ft. 9 in. × 4 ft. (175 ×
122 cm.). Bottom :
Bergama Transylvanian prayer
rug. Early 18th century. 5 ft. 8 in.
× 4 ft. (172.5 × 122 cm.).*

Early nineteenth-century Kula prayer rug of 'tomb' design. 7 ft. × 4 ft. 5 in. (213.5 × 134.5 cm.). Ex-Kevorkian Collection.

*Above: silk carpet based on
a Hereke copy of a Persian
animal carpet. Made by the
Tossounian factory on the island
of Corfu, c. 1930. 5 ft. 9 in. ×
4 ft. 3 in. (175 × 130 cm.).*

Below: mid-nineteenth-century Melas rug. 3 ft. 8 in. × 3 ft. 3 in. (112 × 99 cm.).

Above centre: late eighteenth- or early nineteenth-century Mudjur prayer rug. 5 ft. 10 in. × 4 ft. 7 in. (178 × 140 cm.). Above: nineteenth-century Kirshehir rug. 5 ft. 8 in. × 4 ft. (173 × 122 cm.).

Eighteenth-century Ladik prayer rugs. Top: 6 ft. 2 in. × 3 ft. 7 in. (188 × 109 cm.); above: 5 ft. 2 in. × 3 ft. 5 in. (157 × 104 cm.).

Left: late eighteenth-
or early nineteenth-century
Smyrna rug, possibly woven in
Ushak. 6 ft. 10 in. × 6 ft. 3 in.
(208.5 × 190.5 cm.).
Ex-Kevorkian Collection.

Below left: Bergama rug of
garden design. Early 19th
century. 8 ft. 9 in. × 5 ft. 4 in.
(267 × 162.5 cm.). Below:
Bergama rug with a field showing
the influence of Transylvanian
prayer rugs and border of Kufic
inspiration. Early 19th century.
6 ft. 6 in. × 5 ft. 9 in. (198 ×
175 cm.).

Above: mid-nineteenth-century Melas rug. 3 ft. 8 in. × 3 ft. 3 in. (112 × 99 cm.).

Opposite, top left: nineteenth-century Koum Kapou silk rug of Persian animal carpet design. 6 ft. 10 in. × 4 ft. 4 in. (208.5 × 132 cm.). Opposite, top right: early twentieth-century Koum Kapou silk and metal thread carpet, based on a Persian tile pattern design. 9 ft. 8 in. × 6 ft. 11 in. (295 × 211 cm.). Opposite, bottom left: nineteenth-century Hereke silk and metal thread carpet, the design being of the same type as that of the Salting carpet. 6 ft. 7 in. × 5 ft. 4 in. (200.5 × 162.5 cm.). Opposite, bottom right: early twentieth-century Turkish (Hereke or Istanbul) silk rug of Indo-Persian inspiration. 10 ft. × 3 ft. 3 in. (305 × 99 cm.).

Right: late nineteenth- or early twentieth-century Hereke silk copy of the Ardabil Mosque carpets. 9 ft. 4 in. × 4 ft. 10 in. (284 × 147.5 cm.).

Below, left to right: Yuruk carpet showing the influence of many different styles – Turkoman, Caucasian and Bergama, mid-19th century, 8 ft. 10 in. × 5 ft. 9 in. (269 × 175 cm.);

Left: Bergama rug. Note the similarity of the design to many Caucasian pieces. Late 19th century. 5 ft. 6 in. × 4 ft. 5 in. (167.5 × 134.5 cm.). Above: late nineteenth-century Ezine Bergama rug. 5 ft. 9 in. × 5 ft. 8 in. (175 × 173 cm.).

Above: striped Melas (Karaova Melas) prayer rug. Mid-19th century. 4 ft. 4 in. × 3 ft. 6 in. (132 × 107 cm.).

Above right: mid-nineteenth-century Koum Kapou silk and metal thread carpet of arabesque design. 5 ft. 6 in. × 3 ft. 7 in. (168 × 109 cm.).

Above: eighteenth-century Ghiordes prayer rug with typical horse-shoe mihrab. 5 ft. 8 in. × 4 ft. 5 in. (172.5 × 134.5 cm.). Above right: early eighteenth-century Ghiordes prayer rug of unusual triple-arch form. 5 ft. 7 in. × 4 ft. (170 × 122 cm.).

Left: nineteenth-century Hereke silk carpet of Persian inspiration. 13 ft. 8 in. × 11 ft. 4 in. (417 × 340 cm.).

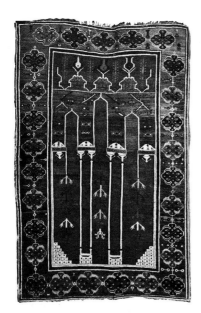

Late seventeenth- or early eighteenth-century triple-column Ladik prayer rug with three unusual candelabra motifs in the mihrab. 5 ft. 4 in. × 3 ft. 5 in. (162.5 × 104 cm.).

Nineteenth-century Çanakkale (Bergama) rug, with a design which echoes that of some of the large pattern Holbein rugs of the 15th and 16th centuries. 5 ft. 8 in. × 3 ft. 3 in. (172.5 × 99 cm.).

Above: early twentieth-century Turkish silk prayer rug: the design is of late sixteenth-century Ottoman inspiration, and the field pattern of the mihrab and the Kufic borders are copied from one of the Seljuk carpets in the Turk ve Islam Museum, Istanbul. 6 ft. 6 in. × 4 ft. 5 in. (198 × 132 cm.).

Later Persian Weaving

IN DISCUSSING weaving in Persia during the 19th and 20th centuries, there are a number of confusing issues. Basically, there are two predominant groups: the tribal village carpets and the urban factory pieces. Names for particular types of carpets do not necessarily refer to the places in which they were woven; they can refer instead to the town in which they were marketed, to a specific design, or to a certain quality of weave; they can even refer to size. In other words, it has to be remembered that for the last 100 years weaving in Persia has been a highly commercial affair, in the hands of dealers and merchants who classify all carpets in terms of merchandise. It has been suggested that the conversion of weaving into such a commercial industry began under the influence of Tabriz merchants in about 1875.

In Tabriz, the Kurdish tribes developed the classic Safavid motifs — such as the garden and tree carpet designs — but in doing so debased the style and coarsened the quality of manufacture. Floral patterns became ever more closely strewn with palmettes, vases and assorted foliage, but the material content deteriorated rapidly...although there were exceptions. Some standards were better maintained in the outlying districts of Herez, west and south of Tabriz, for example. But Hamadan, a region fairly west-central in Persia, can lay claim to even more importance in carpet production; its major towns are Hamadan (itself), Senneh, Bijar, Seraband, Feraghan, Saruk and Derghezan, all in the province of Kurdistan. Pieces known as Hamadans generally have a medallion and escutcheon design, or several such motifs joined by poles; older pieces may have beautiful camel fields and borders. Senneh and Bijar pieces often have a plain field with arches and large medallions and poles at both ends, commonly ending in anchor-shaped escutcheons amid dense floral patterns. From Feraghan and Seraband come good quality carpets generally having a tight all-over field pattern of tiny floral motifs, such as the Herati design; early examples are characterized by a distinctive yellow-green colour.

In central Persia, from Teheran in the north to Kerman in the south, there are equally famous weaving cities: Kashan, Kum, Isfahan, Joshaqan and Yezd, for example. Just outside Isfahan is the region of the formerly nomadic tribe, the Bakhtiari, whose carpets often have medallions or all-over repeat patterns, sometimes within a square lattice. The population of Kashan favoured designs incorporating complex floral patterns arranged in arabesques; they also occasionally went in for cruder pictorial rugs, a few of which portrayed objects of Sufi devotion. Kerman carpets commonly used the *boteh* design, known in England as the Paisley pattern, although in recent times they have presented far less classic motifs. *Botehs* are also a feature of the work of the Asfar tribe, south of Kerman.

The southern Persian province of Fars is the home of the Kashgai tribe who, in their weaving, use a predominantly red palette and incorporate many Caucasian features — such as their favourite pattern of a diamond medallion with a parallel zigzag, or formalzied *botehs* — although they also seem fond of depicting lions. Stylized animals are also common in their high quality work. In the south too are the Khamseh tribe and the weaving city of Shiraz, the latter the home of the so-called 'mille-fleurs' prayer rugs. In such rugs, the mihrab is formed on either side by a half cypress tree and has a scalloped arch within which is a flowering shrub with hundreds of multicoloured flower heads radiating from stems emerging from a central column.

Eastern Persia is occupied mainly by Turkoman and Baluchi tribal nomads.

Persian Carpet Classification

Obviously we have been able to give little more than a general guide to the history of weaving in Persia over the last 175 years. However, probably more Persian carpets come onto the market in the West than any other type, and we feel it would be useful to append here an alphabetical list of names which the prospective purchaser is likely to encounter in visiting dealers. Even such a list as this cannot be comprehensive; we have not, for instance, given all the hundreds of small villages which can only be named as specific sources if there is an incontrovertible provenance, rather than the twenty or thirty other villages in the same area weaving carpets of identical design and quality. Nor have we broken down the tribal weavings into the many sub-groups now known, more of which are being discovered by ethnographers in the field every year. Our list contains only those named which are the most prevalent in the carpet trade today, and have been culled largely from auction and dealers' catalogues of the past few years.

Afshar Tribal rugs from south of Kerman.

Ainabad Kurdish rugs woven in this village in north-west Persia. Often referred to in the trade as Bibikabads (see below).

Arak (*Sultanabad*) Trade name for carpets marketed in that town.

Ardabil Rugs woven in the last thirty years in that town.

Bakshaish Rugs of a Kurdish type woven in this village near Herez.

Bakhtiari Tribal, semi-nomadic rugs, woven near Isfahan.

Bibikabad Kurdish rugs woven in this village near Herez; used also as a general trade name.

Bijar (*Bidjar*) Rugs of Kurdish type woven in this village in north-west Persia.

Birjand Trade name for coarse rugs marketed through Meshed.

Bozchelu (*Borchelu*) Kurdish village rugs woven in this district and marketed through Hamadan.

Derghezin Kurdish rugs woven in this district and marketed through Hamadan.

Dorukhsh (*Dorosh*) Fine early nineteenth-century pieces; modern pieces very poor; area in the Kainat in east Persia.

Feraghan (*Ferahan*) Generic name for fine Kurdish rugs woven in this and surrounding areas.

Gorovan Poor quality rugs woven in the villages near Herez.

Herat Town now in Afghanistan.

Herez Major weaving centre in north-west Persia.

Ingeles Rugs woven in this village and marketed through Hamadan.

Isfahan For modern pieces, this term can denote either rugs woven in the town itself or rugs of a certain quality marketed in Meshed, but not woven in Isfahan.

Jogan (*Jozan*) Rugs woven in this village, close to Malayer, in north-west Persia.

Joshaqan Rugs woven throughout the 18th, 19th and 20th centuries in this town, although in the trade the name is often given to rugs exhibiting particular designs.

Kabutarhang Small town near Hamadan whose weavings are marketed through the latter.

Karaja (*Karadia*) Rugs woven in north-west Persia showing Caucasian influence.

Kashan Major weaving centre in central Persia.

Kashgai Tribal and village rugs of south Persia (Fars).

Kasvin Trade name for a good quality rug woven in Hamadan.

Kerman Major centre in central Persia.

Kermanshah Trade name for a type of rug woven in Kerman. Also a town in the west.

Khorassan Generic name, much abused in the trade, for carpets woven in the eastern province of Persia.

Kum City of central Persia, significant modern weaving industry.

Kurdish Generic name given to weavings of a tribal type from north-west Persia, which do not lend themselves to a more specific nomenclature.

Laristan (*Luristan*) Generic name for the tribal rugs woven in the province above Fars in south Persia.

Laver Kerman Trade name for old type of Kerman rug. Corruption of 'Ravar', where they were woven.

Lilihan Kurdish rugs woven in this village near Arak.

Mahal Trade name for a quality of rug woven around Arak.

Malayer Village near Arak; fine Kurdish weaving.

Mehreban Area near Herez, but used in trade to describe rugs of a particular quality not necessarily woven there.

Meshed Capital city of Khorassan.

Mochtachan (*Mouchtasha*) *Kashan* Carpet from Kashan woven with lamb's wool.

Mosul Trade name for coarse rug of Kurdish type marketed in Hamadan.

Mushkabad Trade name for a type of carpet woven in and around Arak.

Nain City in central Persia; significant modern weaving industry.

Niris (*Neriz*) City in Fars connected with Kashgai weaving.

North-west Persian Generic name for carpets in Kurdish-Caucasian style which have no specific stylistic attributes.

Petag Abbreviation of Persian Carpet Company; active as manufacturers and exporters in Tabriz from about 1900 to 1930.

Ravar Kerman Village near Kerman; either refers to rugs woven there, especially when early, or is used as a trade name for good quality rugs marketed in Kerman.

Saraband Trade name for rugs woven in Arak, especially fine pieces called Mir Sarabands.

Saruk Kurdish rugs of north-west Persia. Used as a generic term. Also used in modern trade to describe new carpets of a floral type made in the area.

Senneh Town near Hamadan; fine Kurdish weaving; often mis-used in the trade.

Serab (*Sarab*) Rugs woven in this village near Herez. Now used as a trade name for certain types of Kashgai weaving, such as Mecca Shiraz.

Souj-Boulak Kurdish rugs from in and around this area in north-west Persia.

Tabriz Capital of Persian Azerbaijan, north-west Persia; important rug weaving and marketing centre.

Teheran Capital of modern Iran; modern rug weaving industry.

Veramin Made in this village near Teheran.

Yezd (*Yazd*) City of central Persia; there is a modern rug weaving industry set up by Tabriz merchants.

Zenjan Trade name for carpets woven in Khamseh district north of Hamadan.

Zeli Sultan Trade name for a type of floral rug woven in Hamadan. This expression can also refer to a particular pattern.

Ziegler Carpets woven for, and designed by, Ziegler's in Sultanabad (Arak) *c.* 1885–1930.

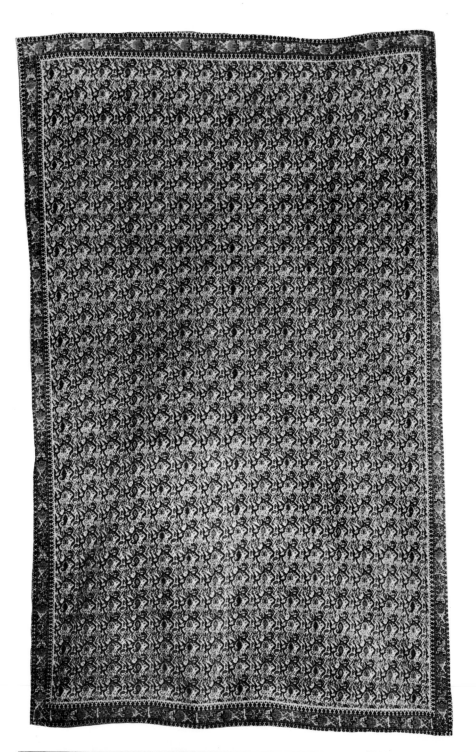

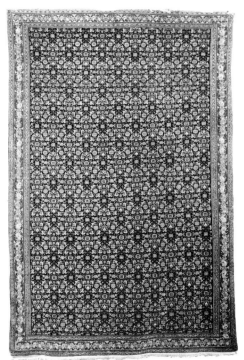

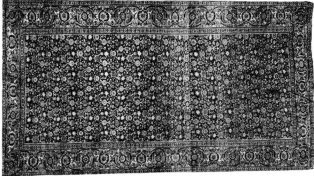

Above: nineteenth-century Herat floral carpet. 9 ft. 4 in. × 4 ft. 11 in. (284 × 150 cm.).

Above: Teheran rug showing 'The Map of Modern Iraq', c. 1920. 5 ft. 10 in. × 4 ft. 9 in. (178 × 145 cm.).

Top left: late nineteenth-century Zeli Sultan rug from the Hamadan region. The carnation and leaf border is characteristic of these carpets. 6 ft. 8 in. × 4 ft. 2 in. (203 × 127 cm.).
Top right: Senneh rug with Herati border, late 19th century. 8 ft. 5 in. × 5 ft. 5 in. (257 × 165 cm.).
Centre right: Senneh rug with plain lozenge centre. Late 19th or early 20th century. 6 ft. 4 in. × 4 ft. 2 in. (193 × 127 cm.).

An outstanding Kashgai rug with
ivory ground. Second half of the
19th century. 4 ft. 6 in. ×
3 ft. 6 in. (137 × 107 cm.).

Opposite: Kerman pictorial
carpet depicting 'The Heavenly
Ascent of Muhammed' from the
Khamsa of Nizami, c. 1900.
10 ft. 7 in. × 7 ft. 2 in. (323 ×
218 cm.).

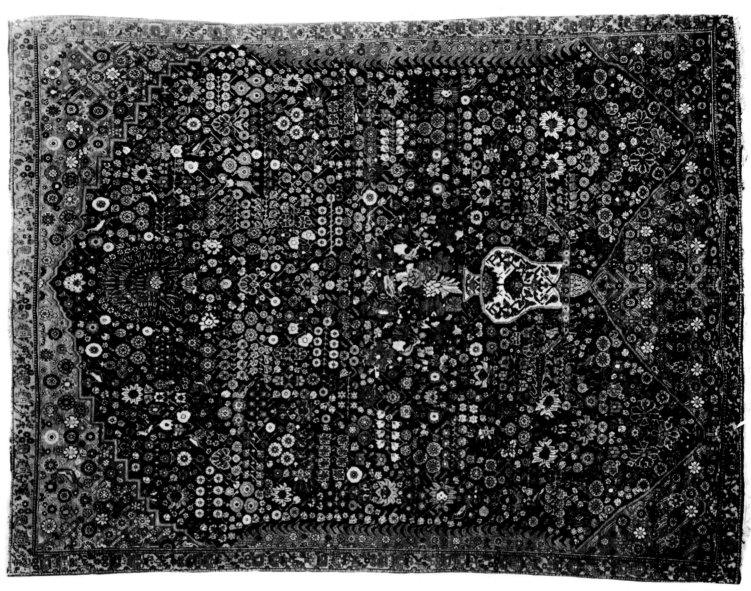

*Above : mille-fleurs prayer
rug. Late 19th century, possibly
Feraghan. Approximately
5 ft. 8 in. × 3 ft. 11 in. (173 ×
119.5 cm.).*

*Opposite, top left : late nineteenth-
or early twentieth-century Tabriz
silk rug, the rust-red field is
decorated with a dedicatory
inscription to Shah Ismael in
Nashki calligraphy, dated
A.H. 926 (A.D. 1509). 6 ft. 2 in.
× 4 ft. 8 in. (188 × 142.5 cm.).*

*Opposite, top right : late
nineteenth- or early twentieth-
century Tabriz silk rug with an
olive green field. 6 ft. 2 in. ×
4 ft. (188 × 137.5 cm.).*

*Opposite, bottom : detail of a
nineteenth-century Tabriz tile
pattern garden carpet. 20 ft. 7 in.
× 13 ft. 10 in. (627 × 422 cm.).*

*One of a pair
of late nineteenth-century
Kashgai saddle-bags. 2 ft. 2 in.
(66 cm.) square.*

*Above: early nineteenth-century
Herez silk carpet of medallion
and arabesque design. 14 ft. 10 in.
× 11 ft. (427 × 335 cm.).*

*Opposite: mille-fleurs Moghul
prayer rug. Late 17th or early
18th century. 5 ft. 4 in. ×
3 ft. 8 in. (163 × 112 cm.).
Ex-Kevorkian Collection.*

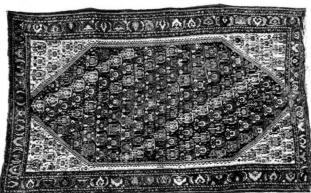

Mid-nineteenth-century Afshar medallion rug. 6 ft. × 4 ft. 8 in. (183 × 142 cm.).

Above right : nineteenth-century Kashgai carpet with triple medallion, 8 ft. 10 in. × 5 ft. 3 in. (269 × 160 cm.). Right : late nineteenth-century Niris floral rug, 8 ft. 3 in. × 4 ft. 9 in. (251 × 145 cm.) ;

Opposite, top left : mid-nineteenth-century Bijar medallion carpet. 8 ft. 9 in. × 5 ft. 9 in. (267 × 175 cm.). Opposite, top right : mid-nineteenth-century Bijar medallion carpet. 18 ft. 5 in. × 11 ft. 5 in. (561.5 × 242.5 cm.) Opposite, bottom left : early nineteenth-century Senneh boteh rug. 6 ft. 8 in. × 4 ft. 4 in. (203 × 132 cm.). Opposite, bottom right : late nineteenth-century Bijar pictorial rug depicting King Hushang, second legendary king of the Shah Nameh. 7 ft. 8 in. × 4 ft. 8 in. (234 × 142 cm.).

Two late nineteenth-century Saruk rugs. Below left : this piece shows a marked similarity in layout to the Safavid Portuguese carpets. 7 ft. 11 in. × 4 ft. 6 in. (241.5 × 137 cm.). Below: rug with an indigo field. 6 ft. 9 in. × 4 ft. 2 in. (206 × 127 cm.).

*Above: Feraghan rug with white
ground with birds, second half of
the 19th century. Approximately
8 ft. 6 in. × 5 ft. 4 in. (259 ×
162.5 cm.). Jay Jones Collection,
California.*

*Above: nineteenth-century pictorial
rug, possibly from north-west Persia, although an
attribution to Anatolia has been suggested.
7 ft. 2 in. × 4 ft. (218 × 122 cm.).*

Above:
nineteenth-century Kashan wool
prayer rug with tree-of-life.
design. 6 ft. 3 in. × 4 ft. 5 in.
(190.5 × 134.5 cm.).

Above: nineteenth-century Feraghan floral rug with a
dark blue field. 5 ft. 9 in. × 4 ft. 6 in. (175.5 ×
137.5 cm.).

Above: Feraghan pictorial rug based on
the reliefs at Persepolis. Mid-19th century.
6 ft. 9 in. × 4 ft. 3 in. (206 × 129.5 cm.).

Above, left to right: Kerman pictorial rug, late 19th century, 7 ft. 1 in. × 4 ft. 10 in. (223 × 147.5 cm.); Kerman pictorial rug, late 19th century, 8 ft. 8 in. × 5 ft. 9 in. (264 × 175.5 cm); Kashan pictorial rug depicting a Sufi prophet, late 19th century, 6 ft. 8 in. × 4 ft. 7 in. (203 × 140 cm.). Right: nineteenth-century silk hunting rug attributed to Kerman, of the type called Kermanshah. 6 ft. 3 in. × 4 ft. 2 in. (190 × 127 cm.). Below: Kerman oval portrait mat depicting President Theodore Roosevelt. Early 20th century. 2 ft. 11 in. × 2 ft. 3 in. (89 × 68.5 cm.).

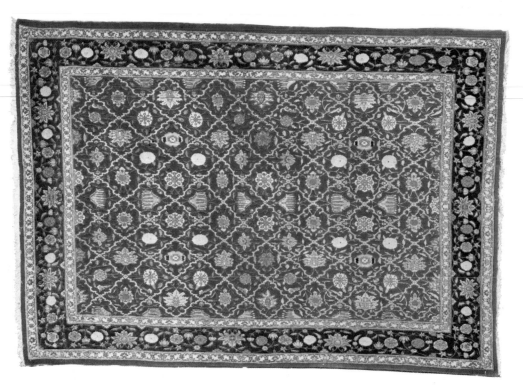

Top: early nineteenth-
century Joshaqan lattice carpet.
Approximately 9 ft. × 6 ft.
(274 × 183 cm.).

Bottom left: detail of an
early nineteenth-century Bijar
carpet. 13 ft. × 4 ft. 5 in. (396
× 134.5 cm.). Bottom
right: late eighteenth- or early
nineteenth-century Bijar carpet.
13 ft. × 4 ft. 5 in. (396 ×
134.5 cm.). The last two carpets
described were formerly in the
Kevorkian Collection.

Opposite:
Isfahan carpet with medallion and
floral arabesques. Late 19th
century. Approximately 9 ft. ×
6 ft. (284 × 183 cm.). Jay Jones
Collection, California.

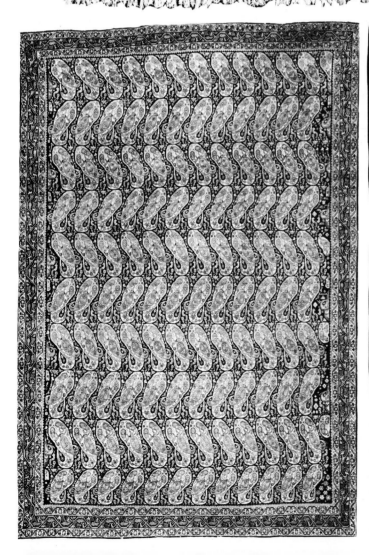

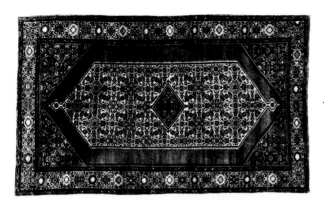

*Above: nineteenth-century
silk Herez rug, with arabesques
and animals. 6 ft. × 5 ft. (183 ×
152 cm.).*

*Opposite: Bakhtiari carpet
inscribed 'Made by the Bakhtiari'
and dated A.H. 1302 (A.D.
1885/6). Approximately 7 ft. ×
5 ft. (214 × 152.5 cm.).*

Top left: nineteenth-century Bijar carpet. 12 ft. 2 in. × 9 ft. (371 × 274 cm.). Top right: Herez silk rug, late 19th century. 9 ft. 3 in. × 6 ft. 2 in. (282 × 188 cm.). Left: an early to mid-nineteenth-century sampler (vagireh) from north-west Persia. 5 ft. 10 in. × 5 ft. 4 in. (178 × 162 cm.). Above: silk-embossed wool rug from Herez, late 19th century. 6 ft. 9 in. × 4 ft. 3 in. (206 × 129.5 cm.).

*Left: twentieth-century
mochtachan (lamb's wool)
Kashan rug. 6 ft. 6 in. ×
4 ft. 3 in. (198 × 129.5 cm.).*

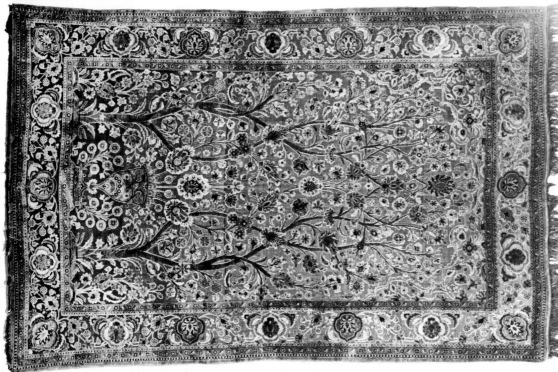

*Late nineteenth- or early
twentieth-century Kashan silk-
embossed prayer rug. 6 ft. 6 in. ×
4 ft. 3 in. (198 × 129.5 cm.).*

*Below, left to right: Saruk
pictorial rug with portrait of
Riza Shah, dated A.H. 1250
(A.D. 1931); 6 ft. 5 in. ×
4 ft. 8 in. (196 × 142 cm.);
Ziegler tree-of-life prayer rug,
late 19th century, 5 ft. 11 in. ×
5 ft. (180 × 152 cm.); very rare
mid-nineteenth-century Herez silk
sampler (vagireh), 1 ft. 6 in. ×
1 ft. 4 in. (45 × 40 cm.).*

Flat Weaving

FLAT-WOVEN ALTERNATIVES to the pile-knotted rug are not confined to any one particular region but are widespread throughout all the countries and tribal groups covered so far. Differentiation between types is by technique. Most common are rugs that are tapestry-woven, called *kelims* in Anatolia, *palas* in the Caucasus, and *sarköy* in Thrace. *Kelims* are often long and narrow, and have the usual carpet layout of field and borders, the field containing large medallions on the long axis surrounded by scattered geometric or stylized floral motifs. A second group of *kelims* comprises prayer rugs which in general follow the designs of pile-woven prayer rugs, particularly those of Konya and Ladik. The *palas* are ordinarily divided into two groups: those from the north, generically called Kuba kelims, and those from the south, called Shirvan kelims. In Kuba kelims the field pattern within the borders consists of either a repeated pattern of stylized animals or large medallions like escutcheons; the Shirvan kelims are closer to Anatolian design.

Another flat-weaving technique is the progressive weft-wrapping method known as *Soumak*, found principally in two types of rug called *sileh* and *verneh*. In most *silehs*, the design consists of rows of large S-shaped motifs in two basic alternating field colours, probably deriving from a highly stylized dragon. *Vernehs* are attributed usually to the south-east Caucasus; the most common form has a madder field on which is an open blue rectangle, all of which is divided into squares by white strips, each square containing geometric motifs and highly stylized birds and animals.

Other techniques are brocading, embroidery and compound-weaving; some rugs combine more than one technique, as do Turkoman bag-faces and tent-bands.

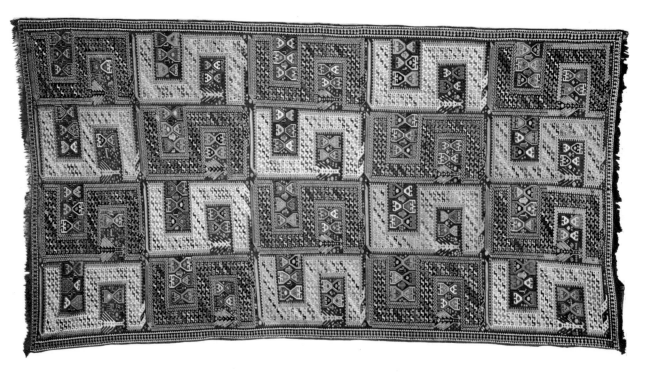

Above: so-called dragon sileh *dating from the mid-19th century. Probably Shirvan. 12 ft. × 6 ft. (366 × 183 cm.).*

Right: dragon Soumak. Probably Kuba or Daghestan, dated 1806. 11 ft. × 7 ft. 6 in. (336 × 229 cm.).

Above: south Caucasian (Shahsevan) verneh *brocaded rug, similar in style to pieces from Akstafa. Mid-19th century. 7 ft. × 4 ft. (214 × 122 cm.).*

Below: pair of Soumak bag-faces. Second half of the 19th century. Approximately 2 ft. (61 cm.) square.

Above: mid-nineteenth-century Shirvan Soumak carpet from the village of Bidjof. 8 ft. 6 in. × 3 ft. 4 in. (259 × 101.5 cm.).

Left: nineteenth-century medallion and jewelled Soumak. Probably Kuba or Daghestan. 10 ft. 8 in. × 6 ft. 4 in. (325 × 193 cm.)

Two so-called dragon silehs, possibly Shirvan. Above left: probably dated A.H. 1258 (A.D. 1843). 9 ft. 3 in. × 6 ft. 2 in. (282 × 188 cm.). Left: second half of the 19th century. 7 ft. 8 in. × 6 ft. 8 in. (234 × 203 cm.).

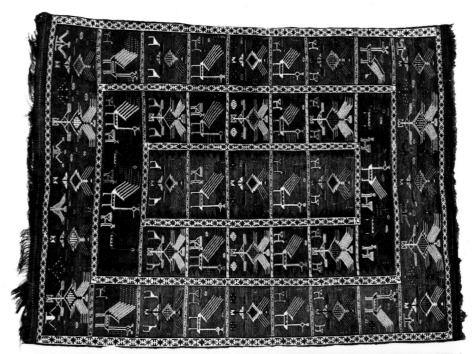

Left: south Caucasian (Shahsevan) verneh *rug, similar in style to pieces from Akstafa. Late 19th century. 5 ft. 11 in. × 4 ft. 6 in. (180.5 × 137 cm.). Below left: nineteenth-century* verneh *brocaded rug. Possibly south-east Caucasus. 5 ft. 7 in. × 5 ft. 2 in. (170 × 157.5 cm.). Ex-McMullan Collection, illustrated in* Islamic Carpets, *no. 60.*

Left , top to bottom: Bokhara suzani *panel, mid-19th century, 8 ft. 10 in. × 7 ft. (269 × 213 cm.); south-west Persian (Fars) kelim, mid-19th century, 8 ft. 6½ in. × 4 ft. 10½ in. (260 × 148 cm.); late nineteenth-century Kashgai kelim, 10 ft. 2 in. × 5 ft. 6 in. (310 × 167.5 cm.).*

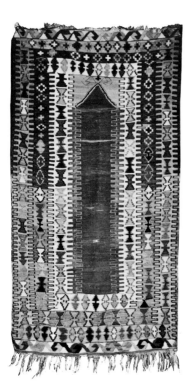

Anatolian prayer kelim. 19th century. Approximately 6 ft. × 3 ft. 8 in. (183 × 112 cm.).

GLOSSARY

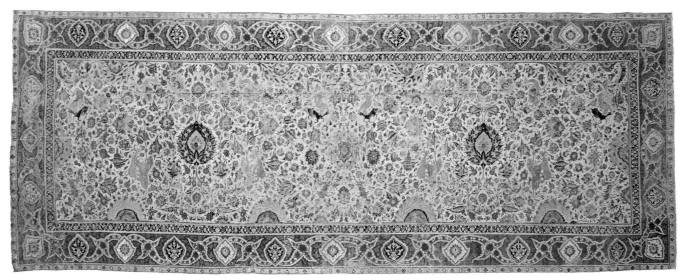

Moghul hunting carpet with white ground. First half of 17th century. Probably Jaipur.
25 ft. × 9 ft. 7 in. (760 × 292 cm.). Islamische Museum, Berlin.

Glossary

Abrash Variations of density in a colour seen in a carpet by irregular horizontal washes; caused by the wool being dyed at different times in different batches of a colour, which is of unequal density. Although an accidental and therefore arbitrary process, *abrash* can greatly enhance the beauty of a carpet.

Ainti Akbari Third part of the *Akbar Nameh*, the *Institutes of Akbar*, which contains a survey of the Moghul Empire.

Akbar Nameh Chronicle of the reign of the Emperor Akbar written by his historian Abu'l-Fazl.

Alum Double sulphate of aluminium and potassium used as a mordant.

Aniline Chemical dye, a derivative of coal-tar. First produced in the 1860s and ubiquitous in the Middle East from the 1880s. Most frequently encountered in the red-blue-purple range, the substance being named after *anil*, the indigo plant. Colours are very fugitive; a bright orange-pink, for instance, will fade at the tip to walnut-brown.

Boteh Widespread pattern of Persian origin (Persian *boteh* = cluster of leaves). Resembles a pear or pine cone, by which names it has been known in the West. Symbolic connections have also been suggested, somewhat fancifully, between it and the Flame of Zoroastra, the imprint of a fist on wet plaster, the loop in the river Jumna, etc. Best known in Europe as the principal motif of the Paisley pattern.

Boteh *motif*

Caliph Head of the Muslim community, with at one time both religious and political supremacy (Arabic, *Khalifat rasul Allah*).

Ch'ang Chinese endless knot. As the inextricable knot of destiny, the seventh of the Eight Buddhist Symbols.

Chinese endless knot

Chinese fret Pattern of interlocking swastikas. Sometimes called the *wan* pattern, *wan* being the Chinese character representing 10,000 (i.e. a swastika).

Chinese fret

Chrome dye A fast synthetic dye mordanted with potassium bichromate. This, and other more recent synthetic colours, are now used in all the major rug weaving areas of the world. Although fast, the colours are harsh and dead.

Cochineal	Scarlet red similar to but more brilliant than lac. Obtained from the crushed bodies of an insect native to Mexico and the West Indies, and imported into Europe from the 16th century (but not into the Middle East until the end of the 18th century). Supposed until the 18th century to be the berry or seed of an oak.
Compound-weave	Technical term for pieces made with more than one set of either warp or weft elements, or both. Form of flat-weaving.
Damascene	After Damascus. Process of decorating steel by etching, inlaying gold or silver, or encrusting, so as to produce a watered effect. In old carpet literature, following European inventories of the 16th and 17th centuries, used to describe either Mamluk carpets or certain designs found on Anatolian pieces. Used either to describe the effect of the design or, as some scholars supposed, because it was believed that the carpets had originated in Damascus.
Diwan	An accounts book or a collection of poems by one author. Also meant a sofa, and thus came to denote a room furnished with such pieces; thus came to mean a council chamber and eventually the council meeting itself.
Djidjim (various spellings)	Refers to either a wall hanging/entrance hanging, or to a weaving technique in which flat-woven strips are joined together to form the completed piece. See the section on flat-weaving.
Ends	The outer edges of the rug on the short axis often woven in the kelim technique (pile-woven ends or skirts are frequently found on Turkoman pieces); the fringes found on carpets are the free ends of the warp threads.
Escutcheon	Shield-shaped medallion often found on Persian carpets as appendages on either side of a large central medallion on the long axis.
Gol Henai Pattern	Floral pattern associated with Persian rugs and said to be based on the Henna shrub (*Lawsonia*); as Edwards has pointed out, more representative of the Garden Balsam, a plant of the genus *Impatiens*. Found frequently on carpets from Hamadan and environs; also found, in schematic form, on Kashgai weavings.
Hejira (or Hijra)	The beginning of the Muhammedan calendar, 16 July, A.D. 622, the date of the Prophet Muhammed's flight from Mecca to Medina. Rugs dated with a year of the Hejira can be converted to the Christian equivalent. For an exact date, divide the Hejira year by 33.7, subtract the result from the original date and then add 622. For an approximate one, simply add 583 to the Hejira date. A number of late nineteenth- and early twentieth-century dated carpets show signs of their dates having been altered so as to make them appear earlier. It was, for instance, an easy process to change 1300 A.H. to 1200 A.H. by altering a few knots. In nineteenth- and twentieth-century dates, the character denoting 1,000 is often omitted, so that the date appears as its last three figures. However, in some instances, the 1,000 symbol is included if the last number of the date is a nought, represented by a dot, which is itself omitted. Thus 121 could equal 1121 (A.D. 1710) or 1210 (A.D. 1796). Late dated carpets, usually Caucasian, often have the Muhammedan and Christian dates woven side by side. Dated Armenian carpets usually have the Christian calendar, and the chronogram of the Gothar carpet is a unique instance. Few carpets dated after 1914 are known.

Herati Pattern   Also called the *mahi* or fish pattern. As its name implies this floral pattern is supposed to have originated in east Persia. Consists of a repeat of a flower head bracketed by two serrate-edged lanceolate leaves. Probably the most frequently used of all Oriental floral designs.

Herati motif

Indigo   Blue dye obtained from the leaves of the indigo plant, one of the various species of *Indigofera*, a tropical genus of *Papilionaceae*. Native to India, from whence most of the leaves used in the preparation of the dye in Persia were exported. The dye was prepared from a fermented compound of crushed indigo leaves, red clay slip, potash, grape sugar and slaked lime.

Jufti   'False' knot, either Turkish or Persian, whereby the knots are tied to four, not two, warp threads, thus coarsening the weave and halving the time involved in production. Became prevalent in Persian in the late 19th century, although for a time it was officially banned.

Kelim   Also spelled kilim, khilim, kileem, gilim, ghilim, gelim, dilim, etc. Form of flat-weaving associated principally with Anatolia. See the section on flat-weaving.

Kermes   Crushed female body of an insect which gives a red similar to cochineal and lac. The insect breeds on the Kermes oak (*Quercus coccifera*). Its use in carpets has never been satisfactorily established.

Koran (Qur'an)   The sacred book of Islam. The Divine Revelations spoken by Allah to His Prophet Muhammed. After the Prophet's death in A.D. 632, the Revelations were passed on orally by *Huffaz*, those who had learned them by heart. In A.D. 633, however, following the death of a number of *Huffaz* in religious wars, it was decided to commit the Revelations to writing. The Koran was therefore compiled by the Prophet's secretary Zayd ibn Thabit and codified by the third Caliph, Uthman, in A.D. 651. This version was then produced in four identical copies which were sent to Mecca, Medina, Basra and Kufa respectively, and which formed the basis of all future manuscripts. The Koran is the literal word of God, and therefore no variations (excepting a few minor ones recognized by Ibn Mujahid and codified in A.D. 933) have ever been admitted; even vowels and accents, representing as they do the speech rhythms of God, must remain uniform.

Kufic   Form of Arabic script; its visual format is used as a decorative motif in the borders of Oriental carpets, especially those from Anatolia. Named after an erroneous ascription to Kufa(h) in Mesopotamia. The principal script of the Koran. Other Arabic or Persian scripts include *al-ma'il*, *nashki* and its variant *nastaliq*, *ta'liq*, *rihani*, *thuluth* and *shikasta*.

Typical Kufic border

Lac (or Laq)   Meaning literally 'hundreds of thousands'. Name given to a brilliant deep purple-red obtained from melting and straining the resinous excretions of the *Tachardia lacca*, a scale insect native to India which covers the twigs of certain trees in a resinous substance for the purpose of immuring the female of the species. The red dye, like that of cochineal and kermes, is the extract of the female bodies of the insect, which in this case are gathered with the resin.

Lampas   A method of weaving so that the pattern is raised in relief against the ground. A form of embroidery.

Madder   Deep red-brown dye extracted from the root of the *Rubia tinctorum* or other *Rubia* plants.

Mina Khani pattern   Floral pattern said to have been named after Mina Khan, although this is certainly apocryphal. Repeat pattern of large palmettes and small white flowers contained in a lattice of stems. Stylized geometrical versions found in certain tribal carpets, such as those of the Baluchi.

Mina khani *motif*

Mordant   Chemical substance with which the wool is treated in order to fix the dye colour. Can itself affect the eventual colour and can be corrosive.

Palas   Caucasian name for kelim.

Palmette   A flower head of heart-shape with many radiating lobes or petals.

Typical palmette

Pomegranate Rind   Gives a dull yellow dye.

Quatrefoil   Medallion with four rounded lobe sections.

Sarköy (or Sharkyoy)   Name for kelims made in Thrace.

Saph   Prayer rug with multiple mihrabs.

Selvedge   The outer warps of the rug on the long sides, which are overcast to form firm braided edges. On many tribal pieces, further strengthened with goat's hair.

Shah Abbas design   Floral design of large palmettes such as those found on the two- and three-plane lattice vase carpets.

Shah Nameh	*The Book of Kings*, an epic of pre-Islamic Persia written by Firdausi of Tus (d. 1020). Many elaborately illustrated (illuminated) copies survive from the 14th, 15th and 16th centuries.
Sileh	(Silé, Sillé, Zilé) Thought to be a corruption of a now unknown Caucasian place name. A form of Soumak, *sileh* usually refers to pieces woven with rows of large S-motifs thought to represent the dragon motif degenerated to virtual abstraction. See section on flat-weaving.
Soumak	(Sumak, Summak, Sumacq, Sumakh). Thought to be a corruption of Shemaka, town in south-east Caucasus. Technique of progressive weft wrapping. See section on flat-weaving.
Spandrels	Architectural term for the space between the curve of an arch and the enclosing mouldings. Thus the space immediately above the arch of the mihrab in a prayer rug.
Swastika	A hooked cross. Chinese symbol for 10,000 (*wan*) and happiness. In many cultures, a symbol of the sun. An extraordinarily ubiquitous symbol, found contemporaneously as far apart as Pre-Columbian America and China, which appears in the work of almost all known cultures.

Typical swastika designs

Tiraz	Official weaving factory usually set up under Royal patronage.
Tchintamani	Chinese Buddhist symbol thought by some scholars to be the origin of the balls-and-stripe motif found on Ushak carpets and other Turkish weavings and textiles.
Verneh	(Verné). Thought to be a corruption of a now unknown Caucasian place name. Technically, these pieces are either Soumak or brocaded rugs (or sometimes a mixture of both), while stylistically the name usually applies to pieces woven with a design of squares, containing either geometric motifs, or a mixture of geometric and animal motifs, especially long-tailed birds.
Vine leaves	Give a yellow dye (as do autumnal apple leaves).
Waqf	The gift from a private individual to a religious institution such as a mosque.
Warp	Longitudinal threads forming part of the foundation of a carpet.
Weft	Latitudinal threads forming part of the foundation of a carpet.
Weld	Extract of the *Reselda lutuola* plant, gives a yellow dye.
Whey	Watery part of milk used in combination with madder to give a particular rose red found on certain Sultanabad carpets.
Yin-Yang	Chinese symbol of the female-male elements. Two interlocked foetal motifs in a circle.

Yin-Yang *symbol*

Acknowledgements

The editor and publishers would like to thank the various museums and other institutions which have provided photographs of carpets in their collections and information about them; and also Christie's in London, Sotheby Parke Bernet in London and New York, Lefèvre and Partners, Raymond Benardout and other dealers and salerooms who have, as usual, been most helpful and cooperative. Special thanks is due to the many individuals who have given us the benefit of their knowledge and experience – above all, David Black and Clive Loveless, partners in one of the most dynamic firms of carpet dealers in London, C. John, Victor Franses, Michael Franses, Jack Franses (now carpet expert at Sotheby's in London), Dr. Jon Thompson, Edmund de Unger, Jackie and Michael Pruskin, Michael Whiteway, Jay Jones of California and many others. The editor would also like to extend his thanks to his fellow authors: Isabelle Anscombe, Harmer Johnson, Gérald Schurr and John Siudmak, the last-named the carpet expert at Christie's, who has also given much help and advice in the preparation of the section on Oriental weaving, and to Anne-Marie Ehrlich for her indefatigable picture research.

The publishers and editor also wish to acknowledge their indebtedness to the owners of copyright in the short passages of quotation in the text, especially to Dr. Joan Allgrove and Dr. May Beattie, to the Metropolitan Museum of New York for permission to quote from *Rugs in the Metropolitan Museum* by M. S. Dimand, to Faber and Faber, London, and the University of California Press for permission to quote from the English-language edition of *Seven Hundred Years of Oriental Carpets* by Kurt Erdmann, and to the Arts Council of Great Britain and Donald King for permission to quote from the catalogue of the *Arts of Islam* exhibition at the Hayward Gallery, London, in 1976.

(t = top; c = centre; b = bottom; l = left; r = right)

David Black Oriental Carpets Ltd 37, 39b, 41b, 44, 45b, 49t, 52tl, tr and b, 53, 57, 59bl, 68br, 71tc, 80, 89, 97, 100, 101tl, tr and b; Collection of the Duke of Buccleuch and Queensberry 7r; Christie, Manson & Woods Ltd 8l, 10t, 11l, 15, 18, 28, 35t, c and br, 38bl, bc and br, 39tl, tr and c, 43 tl, c and br, 51b, 58, 59l and br, 61, 64, 67tr and cr, 71tl, c and bc, 72, 73tr, 74l and cr, 75, 79bl, 83t, 87tr, 90bl, 91tr and br, 95tl and tc, 99t and br, 102b, 103b, 104r; P. & D. Colnaghi & Co., London 12t; Corcoran Gallery of Art, William A. Clark Collection 22r; Hotel Drouot, Paris 30r; Fogg Art Museum, Cambridge, Mass. 12b; Michael Franses 20t, 59bc, 60b, 105; Islamisches Museum, Berlin 19tr, bl and br, 20b, 21, 29; Jay Jones Collection, California 79bc, 88, 93; Kunst und Gewerbe Museum, Hamburg 6; Metropolitan Museum of Art, New York, 7, 14c, 24, 32tl and tr, 36, 45t; Musée des Tissues, Lyons 33br; Museum of Fine Arts, Boston 33l, Österreichisches Museum für angewandte Kunst 33tr; Private Collection 15l; Quarto Publishing Ltd 48, 56; Prince Roman Sanguszko, Paris 6; Shrine Collection, Meshed 14br; Sotheby Parke Bernet 8r, 9, 13, 14br, 16, 17, 19tl, 22l, 25, 26, 27, 31t, 32, 34, 35bl, 38tl, and tr, 41t, 42, 43tr, tc, c, bc and bl, 46, 47, 50, 51tl and tr, 54, 55b, 59tr and bl, 62, 63, 65, 66, 67tl, c and b, 68t and bl, 69, 70, 71tr, bl and br, 73l and b, 74tr and br, 79tl, tc, tr and bc, 81, 82, 83b, 84, 85, 86tl, tr, cl, bl and br, 87tl, bl and br, 90tl, tr and br, 91tl, tc and bl, 92t, bl and bc, 94, 95cl and cr, 96 98, 99c, bl and bc, 102t and c, 103t, 104tl, cl and bl; Spink & Son Ltd 60tl and tr; Textile Museum, Washington 40; Thyssen-Bornemisza Collection, Lugano 30r; Victoria and Albert Museum, Crown Copyright reserved 31b, 32b, 49b.

Special photography: *Techniques and Materials of Oriental Carpet Weaving* by Michael Freeman.